I0437205

COMMUNITY DEVELOPMENT ENTERPRISE
A VEHICLE FOR CONFLICT RESOLUTION

NAZAR AL BAHARNA

DENVER, COLORADO

Outskirts Press, Inc.
http://www.outskirtspress.com

ISBN: 978-1-4787-3225-9

Outskirts Press and the "OP" logo are trademarks belonging to Outskirts Press, Inc.

PRINTED IN THE UNITED STATES OF AMERICA

ACKNOWLEDGMENT

It is with deep gratitude, I express my appreciation to the following persons who participated, contributed, and supported the idea of the community development enterprise right from the beginning: Ella Kay, Liselotte van den Anker, Alexander Kottke, Mary Papageorgiou, and Jana Psarska.

Special thanks goes to Ella Kay who did a wonderful work in editing and proof reading and making the booklet in its final format, and to Liselotte van den Anker, and Alexander Kottke, for their continuous support, and contribution.

TABLE OF CONTENTS

I
INTRODUCTION

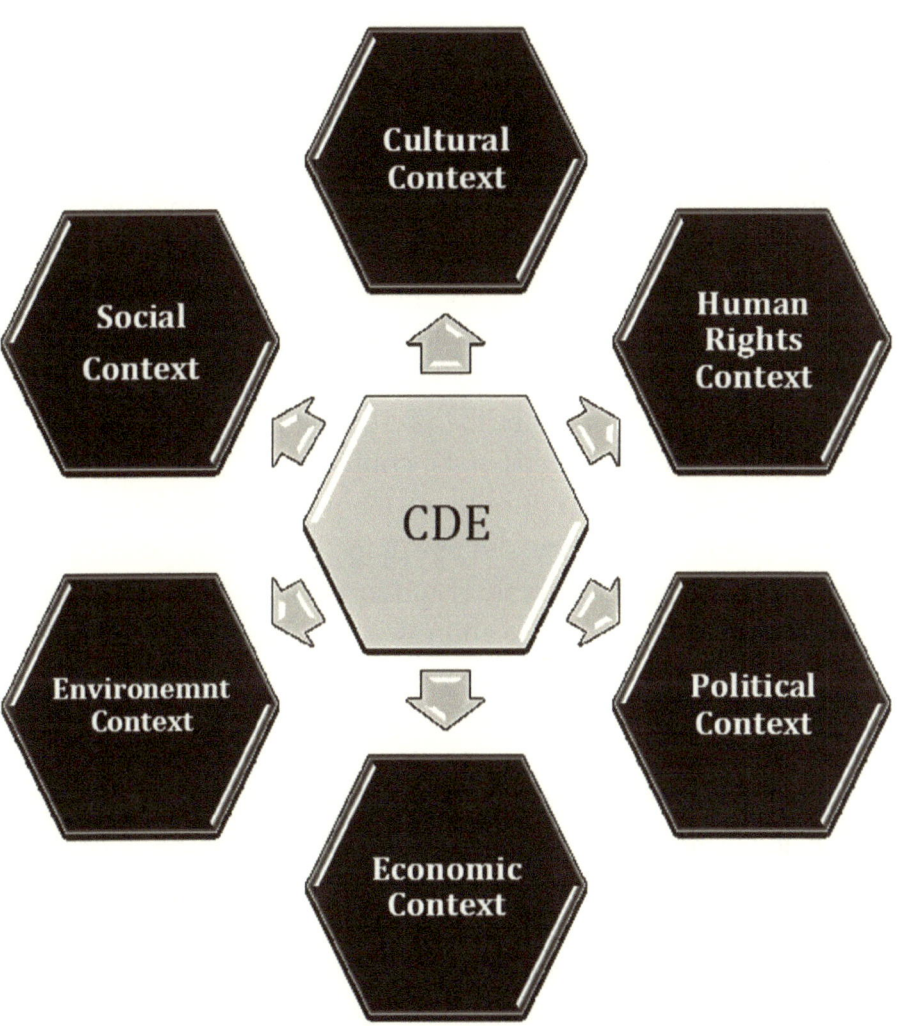

Through history conflicts have tended to be the one of the main precursors for international relations. Today, conflict still remains one of the primary instigators of international action and seems to keep the international community on edge. Old existing conflicts worsen, new conflicts emerge and some conflict situations even improve. A conflict exists when there is an incompatibility between ideology, interests (economic or otherwise) and goals or two or more states. The pursuit of incompatible goals then results in damage to at least one state, with the other state(s) either primarily causing the damage, or intentionally ignoring it. Conflicts are generally solved by forceful intervention or by diplomatic mediation between the respective parties. Historically, most major conflicts have been resolved using forceful intervention. The question remains whether the use of force should constitute an integral part of conflict resolution. Often the threat of external intervention leads to the escalation of conflict rather than resolving it in a holistic way. Moreover, it shifts the focus of the conflict resolution to a political solution rather than prioritizing the people directly affected by the conflict. Therefore, the use of force to resolve conflict is not a sustainable or durable solution because the underlying cause of the conflict is not addressed and the people most affected by the conflict are largely overlooked.

The Community Development Enterprise (CDE) concept hopes to provide a vehicle for the sustainable resolution of conflict by placing the people affected by conflicts at the heart of the solution. For sustainable peace to be achieved the core of the conflict needs to be resolved. The core of most conflicts is often connected to the issues that catalysed the conflict (economic, ideology, etc.) and then exacerbated by the needs of the people affected by the conflict not being met.

Empowering the individual should be the focal point for conflict resolution projects in order to make sustainable outcomes possible. Approaching peoples' needs requires carefully traversing both human rights issues and environmental resource constraints. With these considerations in mind, context specific frameworks should be established whereby individuals in a community will be able to continue to sustain themselves in the long term. As such, the individual should be actively involved in the conflict resolution as well as being the target of effective resolution.

In conflict areas Governments generally execute their plans without direct consultation with the people affected. This causes the relationship between economic and political reforms to be blurred and questionable. Traditional economic indicators (such as GDP per capita, economic growth rate, Human Development Index) do not accurately reflect the needs of the people, or the Government's commitment to human right standards. Accordingly, individuals affected by conflict zones are alienated from active conflict resolution attempts. A Human Rights Based Approach (HRBA) to development should be the foundation for any reform in order for it to be sustainable. A HRBA to development can be defined as an overall framework that integrates the norms, principles, standards and goals of the international human rights framework into the plans and processes of development. The main objective of a HRBA is to empower people through an inclusive and participatory approach, which is focused on 'rights' rather than on 'needs'. A HRBA assesses inequalities that lie at the core of development problems and aims to reform discrimination practices and unjust distributions of power that hinder development growth. The main premise of such an approach is the realization that protection of human rights and sustainable development are mutually dependent, and one cannot be achieved without the other. A HRBA to development emphasizes the importance of involving the people affected by the conflict so that development frameworks established during resolution can be context specific and effectively reflect the identity and rights of the individuals.

Furthermore, a stabilized economy is important for the broader stability of a country. The reconstruction and development of infrastructure in countries that have experienced a severe conflict is merely a technical task that requires a deep understanding of socioeconomic and physical elements over a long-term stabilization processes. Development is increasingly directed towards the need for community driven strategies that can catalyze economic growth. Ideally, an economic plan for post-conflict countries should be based on sustainable development processes and a commitment to fundamental human rights in the rebuilding process.

The proposed solution to conflict is to create an approach that is committed to broader sustainable development principles and a HRBA. This will be done through establishing CDEs in relevant conflict zones, designed to focus on community development and combine social and economic development. It will be directed towards the progress of communities and regions so that the whole population can eventually be benefited. The CDEs will operate to resolve conflicts by directing energy towards the following areas: Human Rights, Social, Economical, Environmental, Political, and Cultural. To enable development in these areas an all-encompassing enterprise will be formed to aid stability and add value in post-conflict zones.

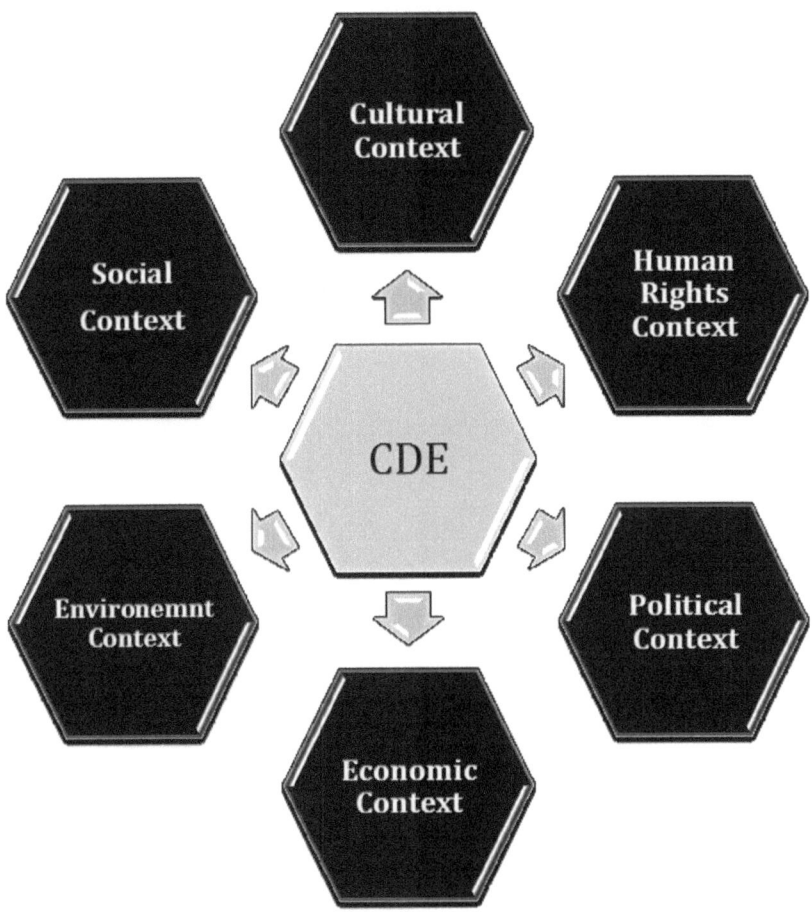

Solving Local Conflicts by Creating CDE

CDEs will be long-term prosperous companies that will enable the societies and the individuals encompassed by them. Two key characteristics of the CDE are participation and inclusion, so the CDE will effectively play an integral role in the community. By allowing the people to have a say in the enterprise's projects and goals, the CDE will facilitate the society's transition to a more democratic and participatory system. In time the CDE will also become a market that can work for the people and feed into the broader community. A major challenge for the CDE is to achieve human development so that economic growth can reach all socioeconomic levels.

II
COMMUNITY DEVELOPMENT ENTERPRISE, CDE

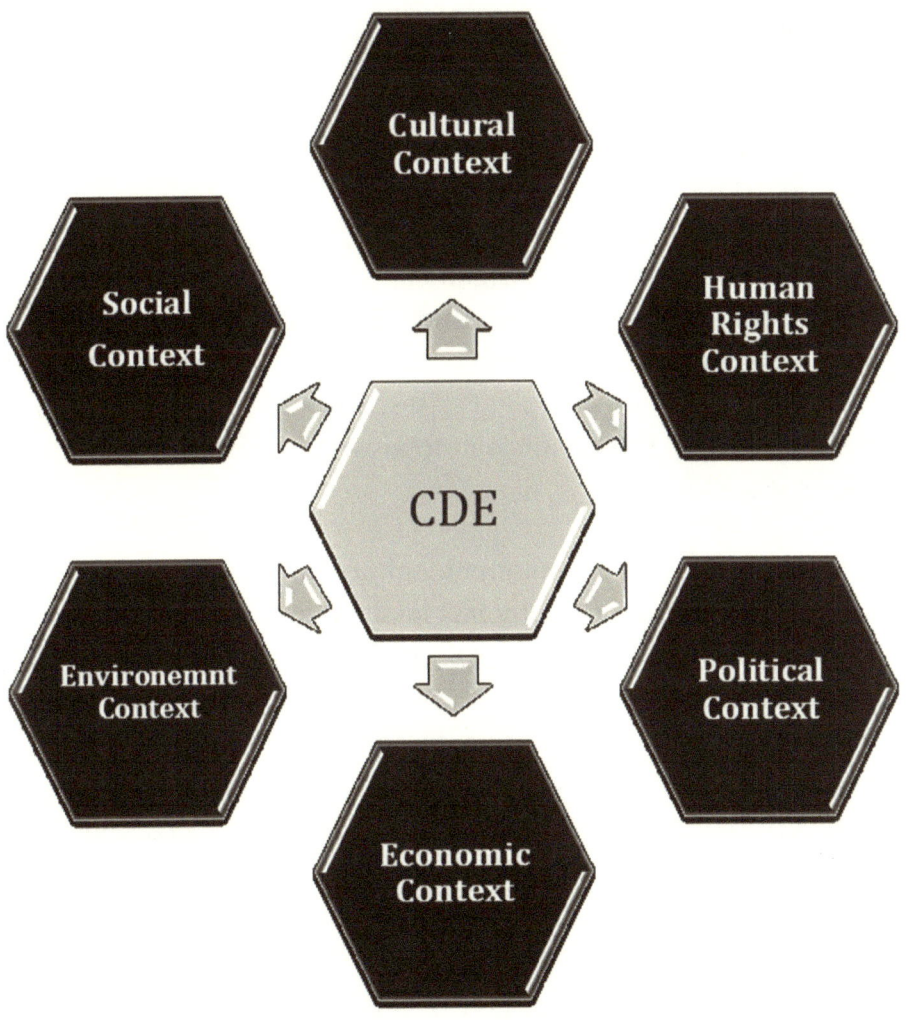

1. CONTEXT

The post Cold War period saw the emergence of armed conflicts, the transformation of the concept of international security and the deepening of economic inequality and social exclusion. The global community has been reformed through an international convergence of agendas on topics such as peace, security and development. Focus has been placed on individuals and communities with the evolution of concepts such as human security, a HRBA to development and the 'responsibility to protect' norm.

Evidence of such global phenomena can be identified through the observation of conflict trends in recent years. After nearly two decades of decline, the numbers of conflict have begun to increase. Research shows that in 2012, a total of 396 conflicts were counted, marking a significant rise from 2011. Among these conflicts were 18 wars and 25 limited wars, indicating that there were 43 highly violent conflicts. Another 165 conflicts were classified as violent crises. So in 2012, a total of 208 conflicts out of 396 conflicts in total were conducted with the use of violence.

Causes of internal and international conflicts are highly complex. Conflicts can generally be classified in a number of ways, such as resource-based conflicts, conflicts over governance and authority, ideological conflicts, and identity (including ethnic) conflicts. The most frequent conflicts in 2012 were system/ideology conflicts (130 cases out of 396 conflicts). Most of the conflicts that come within this category were conducted in order to change the political or economical system, or concerned ideological differences. National power ranked second with 88, followed by resources based conflicts with 81 cases. [Note that many conflicts are centered on more than one conflict item].

In order to provide a sufficient level of human security it is necessary to promote peaceful changes. Decentralized governance can contribute to securing peace and stability in a region. Decentralization has the ability to transform a conflict, bring about power sharing and provide inclusion incentives for minority groups. The concept of decentralization is used here in a broad sense, including the relocation of competences within central institutions (de-concentration) alongside the transfer of some specific tasks to the private sector (deregulation) and to non-central governmental institutions (devolution). The CDE concept can be seen as a form of decentralized governance that is used as a conflict resolution tool specifically designed to focus on community, social and economic development. Furthermore, the CDE is an appropriate forum to implement development initiatives in post-conflict countries.

2. OBJECTIVE

The objective of the CDE is to serve as a vehicle for development and change, as well as on-going stability and peace. The CDE approach will focus on three elements in order to promote peaceful social change, namely: (i) democratization and institutional design, (ii) sustainable development and (iii) good governance. Democratization will focus on the resolution of potential disputes by public participating, thereby achieving a fully democratic process. The sustainable development focus will pay attention to structural changes by seeking to reduce imbalances, improve the welfare of individuals, communities and social groups and reduce the maximum inequality and social exclusion wherever possible. The last element is good governance, which includes various incentives for political in-clusion and power sharing arrangements. By establishing a CDE the people in the community will be able to progressively gov-ern themselves, plan their own development goals and partici-pate in decision-making related to their basic needs. They will be empowered to fulfil their own form of democracy based on their culture and values, at their own pace.

3. WHAT IS A CDE?

In order to explain the concept of the CDE approach, it is neces-sary to provide a clear definition of a Community Development Enterprise. A CDE can be defined as *"a company constituted by democratically chosen people from the prospective community, which is self-sufficient, and takes over the participation from the state in the fields of political, economic and social activities."* Through cooperation and consultation with the government and other international organizations, the CDE will seek to de-velop the community in a way that is sustainable.

The holistic approach of the CDE process will ensure a shift from centralized development to community development. When establishing CDEs, an analysis of the problems in communities will be necessary in order to tailor appropriate responses. The nature of conflict and post-conflict environments is particularly contextual so each community will likely need a different re-sponse from the CDE concept. Successful implementation of the CDE concept will require fine balancing, constant adjust-ment and a spirit of conciliation. Conflict is by its very nature dynamic and unpredictable. Therefore, every intervention to prevent, manage or resolve conflict must be flexible and adapt-ed to the specific needs at a ground level, and not according to institutional set-ups. Different regions, societies and groups tend to prefer different diplomatic approaches. Cooperation with regional and sub-regional organizations is essential, as they have a unique influence and access to crisis situations within their regions. In some regions independent actors that are not affiliated with larger institutions will have comparative advantages that others do not. Engagement is more likely to succeed if it adopts local preferences and remains flexible, while pursuing clear objectives. As such, CDEs will effectively act as a grassroots response to local issues.

4. ADVANTAGES OF THE CDE CONCEPT

The CDE concept takes a holistic approach towards development and enables communities to govern themselves. Communities can essentially work sustainably to achieve broad community objectives in a democratic way. Community development also encourages the society to embrace principles of sustainability, competitiveness and fairness to ensure that each citizen can aim towards their own goals in a secure environment. Community development provides knowledge about respective cultures in conflict zones and helps organizations to work together to efficiently resolve social development issues. The implementation of a CDE will have a "springboard function" in the community to foster change. It can be a stepping-stone for open employment as well as an esteem enhancement for the community's population. Finally, a CDE is a platform for government, private and other sectors to work together with the goal of creating sustainable development. The long-term goals of the CDE concept are to encourage new initiatives, provide financial assistance and business planning, create employment opportunities and promote clean rural environments in under-resourced areas.

Through utilizing devolution as a conflict management tool the CDE concept has advantages such as efficiency, equity, service provision and participation. If properly structured, the CDE approach could improve procedural and distributional equity and increase administrative efficiency and good governance. The CDE approach will also contribute to enhanced popular participation. Accordingly, the CDE has a significant conflict mitigating potential in contexts where it will be successfully implemented. Some key advantages of the CDE approach are:

- Political inclusion of new groups: Decentralization could allow participation of minority groups in political processes in their immediate environment. These groups are often excluded from power at the national level so their direct involvement will achieve more seamless development and ultimately aid the prevention of conflict.

- Deepening of democracy as a means of national integration: The CDE approach could serve as an institutional mechanism to bring sub-national groups into a formal bargaining process with the government. National cohesion and central control are further advantages.

- State legitimation: The CDE approach could be used to achieve state legitimation. The focus will be turned towards meeting the needs of individuals, which will eventually help to achieve in popular support.

Ultimately, the CDE concept brings an approach that is different from other conflict resolution initiatives because it is malleable. CDEs will be established in such a way that adopts the individual factors of conflict situations with a heightened level of perception of cultural, religious and historical aspects. Therefore, the approach to conflict resolution presented by the CDE concept is one with deepened understanding and capacity to absorb different key factors.

III
CDE STRATEGY

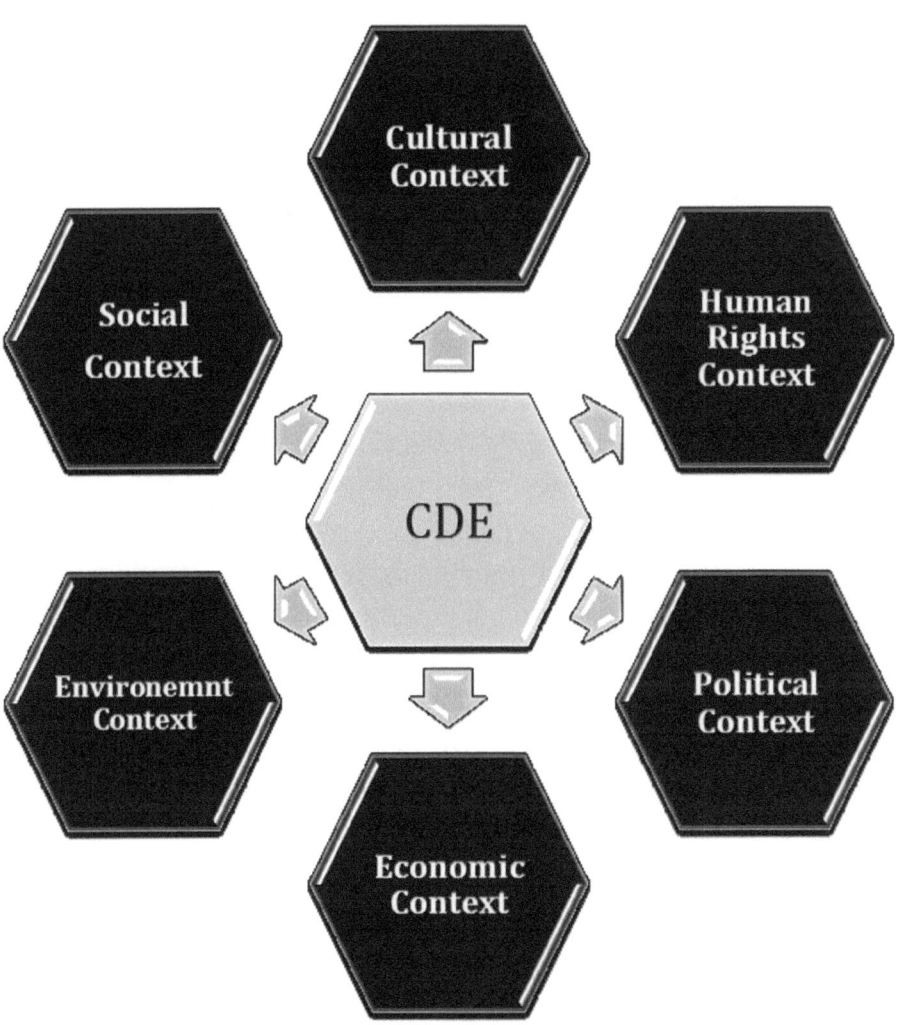

1. ECONOMIC CONTEXT

Conflict and post conflict states introduce an economic context that is generally void of appropriate structure and stability. Every conflict situation is different, presenting a varying range of complexity and intensity. However, economic issues that are common to most conflict situations are linked to the provision and availability of basic goods and inflation of the local currency. These issues can be drawn from anywhere, ranging from the disintegration of domestic government infrastructure to the breakdown of relationships with other states and the imposition of trade restrictions. Economies that have been impacted by conflict present a vulnerable landscape that must be navigated carefully.

The CDE concept responds to the economic facet of conflict by coupling decentralization with microeconomic ideas. The proposed solution is one that takes the pressure off a centralized government as the sole body responsible for placing the country back on its feet. Rather, focus will be shifted towards developing CDEs based on financial strategies that are tailored to the resources and goals of individual communities. Introducing a decentralized approach that operates within the framework of a business or enterprise model is an effective way to re-establish the economy and access the potential of individual communities. This way, development will have a better chance of permanence because it will be formed pertaining to the context of each CDE in each community situation.

2. FINANCIAL STRATEGY

The CDE is intended to be financially self sufficient, which makes it an attractive option for conflict resolution and development.

Initially financial support will need to be injected to establish the CDE in a given context. However, once the relevant infrastructure is in place the CDE will be able to sustain itself. Creating a specific financial strategy for each community will be a matter of research and understanding the broader situation affecting that community. Broadly speaking, the CDE will maintain a relatively conservative financial strategy based on developing capital for future growth and development of service activities and capacities.

3. CDE MARKET ANALYSIS SUMMARY

The CDE is directly involved in developing and providing services to the market and will seek to establish itself as a viable trading organization. The target group on the demand side would ideally be a group of existing and future social enterprises working at the local level with community support and willing to engage with other stakeholders according to the vision and objectives of the CDE. On the supply side, the target group consists of government and private sector institutions that can provide assistance to the target groups in various forms. The CDE concept will aim to facilitate equilibrium between the demand coming from the individuals in a community and the availability of assistance from the supply side.

4. MARKET SEGMENTATION

The CDE will operate alongside the following market segments:

- Government Ministries and Public Sector Entities: This will represent the core initial target of the CDE by providing ample opportunities as government organizations seek to enhance efficiency and improve service channelling to the public.

- Private Sector Establishments and Companies: Private sector partnerships will bring added value to the services offered and will open up more opportunities for the partners of the CDE.

- Members of the community: Community buy-in is very vital so as to meet social objectives that underlie the CDE's philosophy.

5. STRATEGIC ALLIANCES

Various government bodies, NGOs and/or private institutions could partner with the CDE depending on the nature and needs of a given community, and the context of the conflict affecting it. The CDE will aim to align itself with bodies that will enhance the CDE's activities.

IV
CDE SERVICES

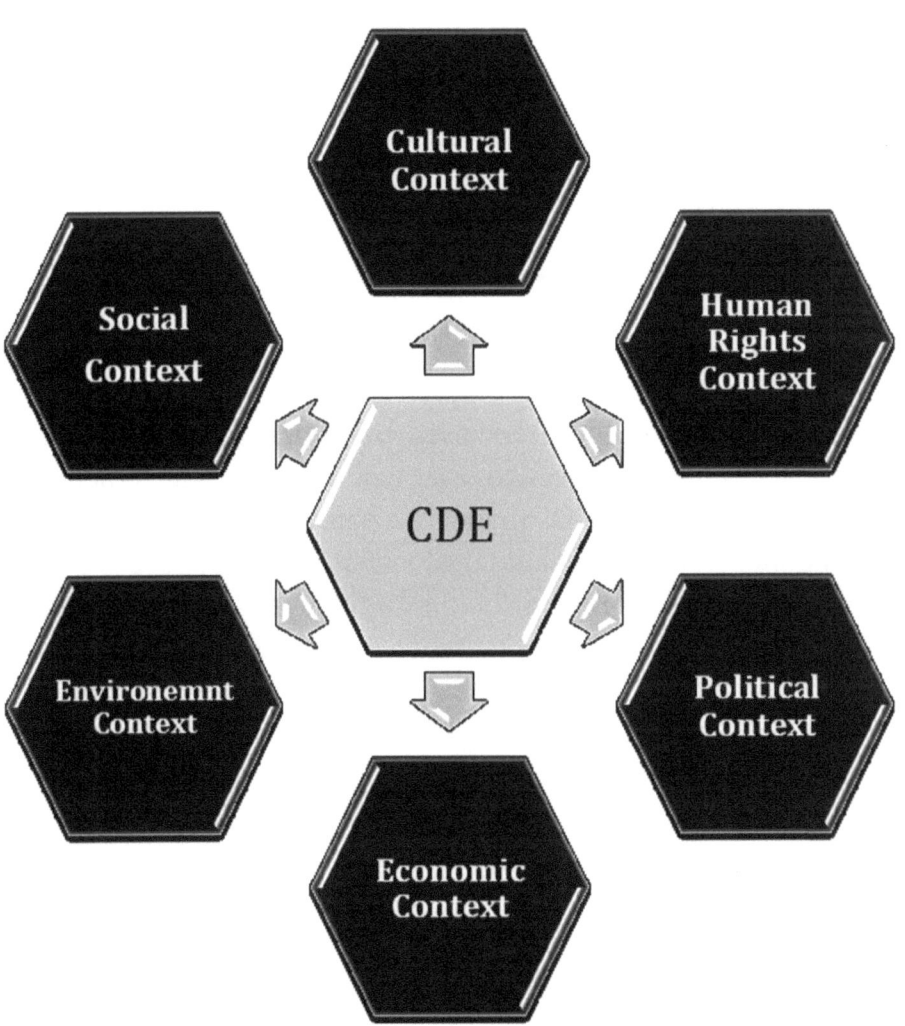

The value of the CDE comes from the desire to create broader ownership for development and reduce gaps in wealth. This notion extends to an awareness of the gap between development plans and cultural and environmental concerns. To varying degrees every country experiences such gaps, and economic growth is necessary but not sufficient for closing them. The proper response is one that extends to the social, economic, cultural and governmental sides of a society. The CDE initiative is a step in this direction, and engages with several relevant aspects of rebuilding a conflict zone in the services it aims to facilitate.

1. SOCIAL, ECONOMIC AND CULTURAL SERVICES

(a) Overview

Development should be achieved by bringing together communities to realize objectives that will determine the structure and operation of the CDE model in a particular context. Service components could include residential complexes, environmentally friendly projects, cultural initiatives and social welfare projects. Broad social, environmental and cultural services facilitated by the CDE may include support of local projects, up-skilling community members to enhance their employment prospects and empowering womens' involvement in projects.

In an economic sense the CDE will act as a supervisory body that will direct business and trading operations. Ultimately, the establishment of CDE frameworks will generate local economies based on fair competition and will integrate local business into the community. Context specific operations will be established through the CDE to achieve financial viability as well as broader economic objectives. Service components will include establishing trade opportunities and investment projects, supporting the financing of projects and providing incubators to encourage individuals to undertake development initiatives.

(b) Application

The idea of establishing a CDE reflects and anticipates the needs of groups who are generally left behind in the process of growth. It aims to enable less fortunate groups to catch up, so that they may consider themselves a significant part of change and the fulfilment of a national vision. The CDE will facilitate these groups to internalize the benefits of development through capital, skills, systems and the will of the nation. This will give ongoing development efforts more permanence because individuals will not experience dissatisfaction. A distinguishing feature of the CDE is that it has a particular social purpose to achieve an overall benefit for the community. In its work the CDE will impact people, the environment and the local economy. The initiatives that will be implemented will be dependent on the individual context of a given community. Some examples of initiatives include:

- Strengthening the social safety net for the disadvantaged and gradually shifting aid from cash assistance to social investment.

- Developing and implementing policies to ensure that social welfare programs target individuals most in need.

- Increasing legal protection, particularly against discrimination.

- Supporting awareness for womens' rights and creating equal opportunities for women in all sectors.

- Abetting low unemployment rates through training programs designed to reintegrate the unemployed into the workforce.

- Establishing programs to address causes of family distress. This could extend to include recreational and financial assistance, and economic empowerment schemes for families.

2. GOVERNMENT SERVICES

(a) Overview

The CDE should develop and implement smarter service delivery arrangements across all government sectors, with a focus on innovation. Efficiency and fairness will also be improved by ensuring that governments are transparent. To this end, bureaucratic employees should be well qualified, and their performance should be continuously evaluated. The adoption of different approaches to service delivery could include more efficient processes, changes to organizational arrangements and the greater use of information technology. Encompassing these changes will enhance the broader efficiency of Government services and insure the long-term effectiveness of development facilitated through the CDE concept.

(b) Application

Government policies, resources and institutions would have

the potential to achieve goals more effectively if they could be linked to the communities where the intended beneficiaries are. A well-designed community institution is a cost effective mechanism for enhancing the outreach and depth of public services. Accordingly, the CDE concept aims to bring together government ministries and NGOs to offer services and benefits together through accessible, personalized services. Service components could include training, employment licensing frameworks, legal advice, counselling, business guidance or events management. The combination of services provided would be pertaining to the particular context of a prospective conflict zone and the needs of the people affected. The Government could also outsource some of its ministerial operations to the CDE, such as operating schools, municipal works and others.

The Government will remain the primary legislator. The government will therefore be responsible for putting the required guidelines in place and establishing the standards for quality of services. The government will outsource certain functions to the CDE. This outsourcing of Government services will be divided into two parts: the service aspects (issuing of relevant trade licenses and permits), and the operational side (e.g. operating schools and health clinics). The following is a list of potential Government areas that could be outsourced to the CDE:

- Education and Health Care: The CDE could be responsible for operating and managing schools and health clinics within the community. This would include the management of existing government schools and health care centres, and the planning and construction of new schools and health care centres should the community require this.

- Utilities (Energy, Water, Sewerage, Roading): The CDE could be responsible for the maintenance of electricity, water, sewerage and roading infrastructures within the community. The CDE could collect utility levies on behalf of the Government.

- Housing: The CDE could be responsible for building affordable housing in the community with the support of the Government and by drawing on available labour.

V
CDE STRUCTURE

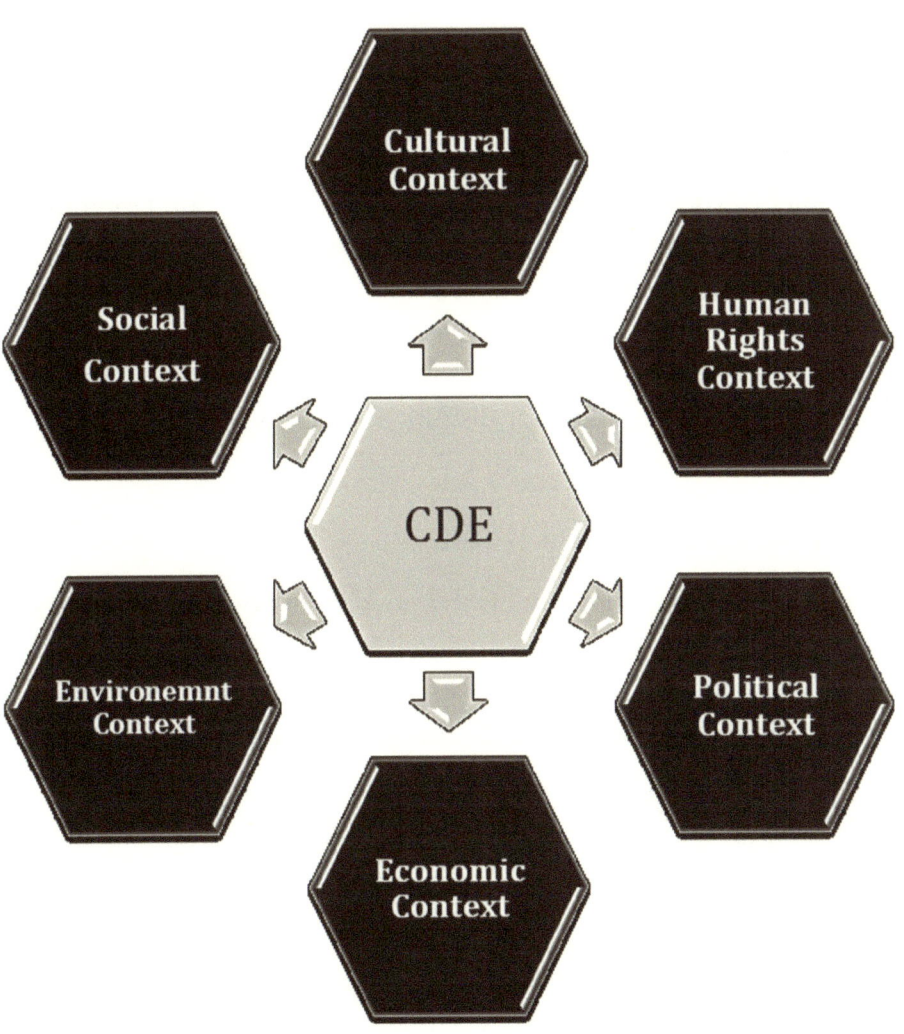

1. OWNERSHIP

The success of CDE relies on how it is will be promoted in the local community and how it will be governed. The CDE will be 90% owned by the people in the community and 10% owned by the Government, regardless of the degree of financial investment from the Government.

2. GENERAL ASSEMBLY

The General Assembly of the CDE represents the highest governing body to oversee the CDE activities. Each voting member in the community (18 years old or above) is entitled to one single free share making him/her a shareholder and member of the General Assembly. The General Assembly has the power to approve and confirm changes to policies, approve annual budgets and dividends, and elect or dismiss any office holder.

3. BOARD OF DIRECTORS

The CDE board of directors is the governing body that oversees the performance of CDE to ensure it is achieving its objectives. The size of the Board of Directors will depend on the size of the CDE and the relevant projects of a given community.

(a) Responsibilities

The responsibilities of the Board of Directors are to oversee the performance of the CDE and to ensure that it is meeting its objectives and the aspirations of the community. The responsibilities of the Board of Directors will be divided among members of the board according to development areas (i.e. Education,

Health Care, etc.)

(b) Election and Voting

The General Assembly of shareholders in a given community will vote to elect the Board of Directors for a term of four years. Votes will be based on one vote per person. The Board of Directors nominees should fulfil a certain criteria, including experience and expertise in relevant areas of the CDE.

4. ORGANIZATIONAL STRUCTURE

The CDE will be structured to include a Board of Directors, CEO, Executive Management and Professionals. It will be an autonomous organization with governance and ownership structures based on participation by stakeholder groups (i.e. users or clients, local community groups, etc.)

(a) Fundamental elements:

- Chief Executive: Will hold the overall responsibility for discharging the CDE's mandate according to particular aims and objectives.

- Vice President for each of the major services: Will have the responsibility to implement the CDE strategy for the relevant community. Note that the categories for Vice President are not closed and will depend largely on the direction of the individual CDE.

- Partnership Unit: Comprised of a Partnership Manager, Research Officer and Field Assistant. Together these roles will assist the respective Vice Presidents in pursuing partnerships and take the lead in documenting stakeholder experiences that highlight success stories and best practices.

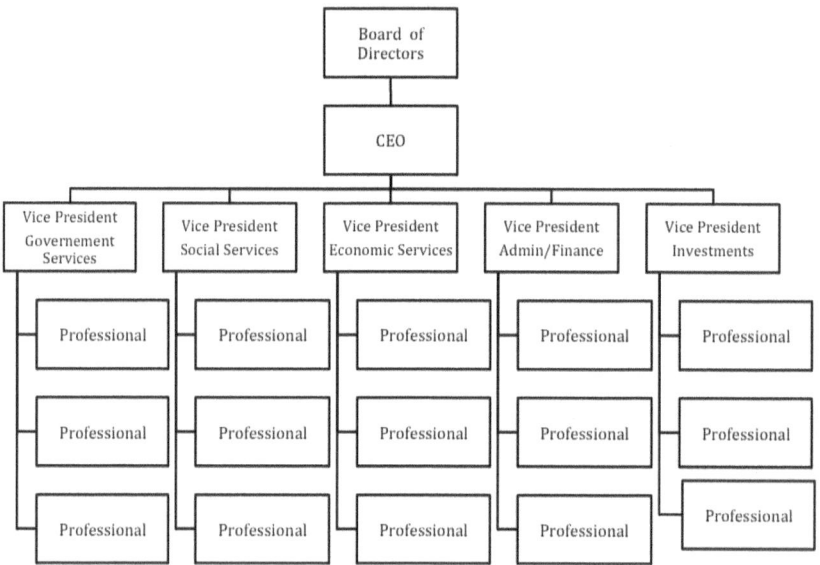

CDE Organization

(b) Additional Elements:

The following aspects will underlie the core CDE organizational structure to ensure efficiency and effectiveness:

- Management Team: Comprised of consulting, marketing and sales experts with contacts and experience working with governments and private sector entities.

- Sourcing: The primary operations of the CDE will be undertaken by a dedicated full-time team of skilled professionals who are representatives from different government bodies with expertise in the various services provided by the CDE.

- Technology: The CDE will be required to adopt a technology-based infrastructure with strong IT support to manage and facilitate CDE operations. The technology will be required to facilitate an effective payment system, efficient Internet accessibility, data processing and presentation facilities (amongst others).

5. COMMUNITY DEVELOPMENT ENTERPRISE HOLDING

In order to spread the CDE concept and manage a larger area, a holding company will be formed with the responsibility of maintaining and implementing CDEs in a given country. The main objective of the Community Development Enterprise Holding (CDEH) will be to integrate the various CDEs toward a unified development plan for the country. It will aim at avoiding duplication and enhancing resources to achieve broader objectives across a given conflict zone.

The CDEH will be a national-level enterprise, and will not be involved in the day-to-day management of the local CDEs. It will deal with policy matters such as equitable distribution of Government support across local CDEs, avoiding overlaps, promoting integration and guiding the local CDEs on issues of sustainable development. The CDEH will be owned by the Government.

The main functions of the CDEH are:

- Directing government resources equitably for local CDE development.

- Avoiding overlap in specializations between CDEs.

- Promoting the integration of CDEs across the country.

- Ensuring compliance with the Government policies across all CDEs, including policy directives for financial sustainability and social responsiveness.

- Obtaining Government support and nurturing an enabling environment for CDEs.

- Investing in local CDEs to assist the creation and growth of local social enterprises in selected parts of the country.

- Advising local CDEs on socially and environmentally sustainable development and maintaining their accountability to financial, social and environmental standards.

- Fusing development initiatives, capital and technical resources over groups of businesses.

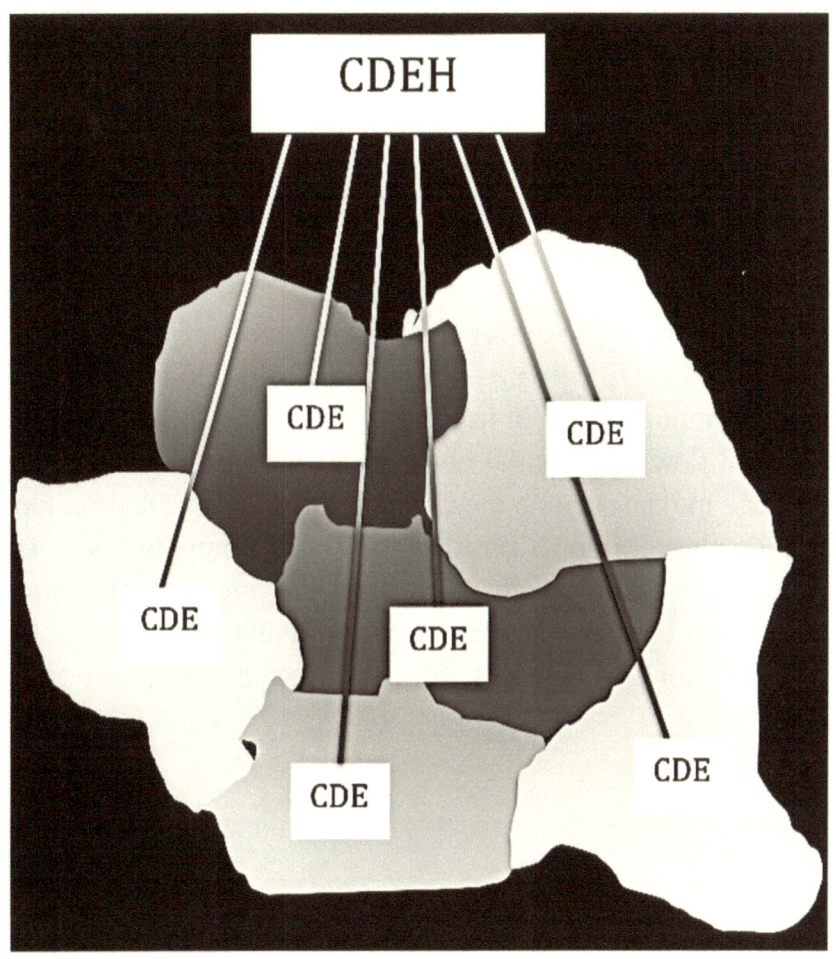

The Relationship Between the CDE and the CDEH

(a) Board of Directors

The CDEH Board of Directors is the governing body to oversee the performance of the CDEH and ensure that it is meeting its objectives. The Board will be composed of one representative from each CDE, alongside Government representatives and representatives from the private sector. The key responsibility of the Board of Directors is to certify that the performance of the CDEH is in line with the broader aspirations of the country.

6. PROTOTYPE

The CDE should be initially prototyped in one or two areas before expanding to cover the entire region of the intended country. The CDE will attract high attention as the first holistic development provider of its kind in a country. This will lead to a natural flow of potential business as word of mouth and experience in dealing with the CDE increases. The CDE prototype will ideally be able to position itself as a competent service-channelling agent, which may attract the attention of a number of other communities. Effective marketing alongside public/private sector engagements will enhance the perception of the CDE.

VI
PROCESS OF
ESTABLISHMENT

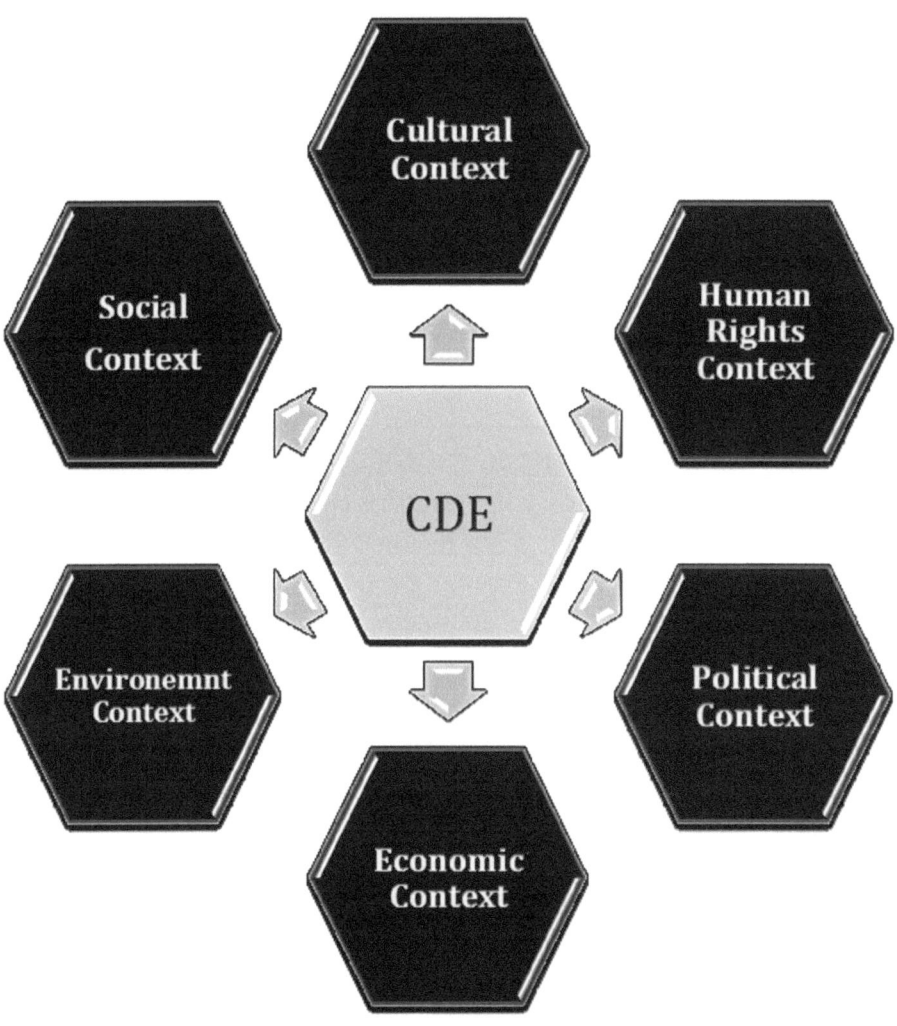

1. OVERVIEW

The Government will outsource the bulk of governmental services to the CDE under the general assumption that people who live in the community itself will be more familiar with the community's individual needs. The engagement of the community will bring vitality and synergy to development aims as well as help to facilitate and manage change. The nature of eligible projects could include, but is not limited to: the promotion of culture and art, addressing social development issues within the community, the proliferation of education, the support of research on issues concerning the community and programs addressing the community's specific identity. Ultimately, new initiatives and activities within the community will be encouraged, and a clear indication of the needs and requirements of the community will be sought.

The proposed CDE concept will be based on three criteria. First, the CDE will work towards financial viability without continuing subsidies. (Note that, the proposed scheme is not intended to be an exception to the country's competitive market economy). Second, the CDE should ensure community buy-in and meet broader social objectives. Third, the CDE should be linked to, and supported by ongoing government initiatives and programs.

2. THE COMMUNITY DEVELOPMENT ENTERPRISE CONCEPT AS A VEHICLE FOR REFORM

Cohesive reforms require dealing with challenges comprehensively and systematically. Reform is a sequential and continuous process that operates in a multi-tier framework. As such, a change on one level may need to be augmented by changes on other levels. Reform requires the careful traversing of political hierarchies, progressive policies, the judiciary system, social establishments and underlying cultural aspects. The CDE will function as a vehicle for effective reform due to its flexible and contextual nature.

3. APPLYING A HUMAN RIGHTS BASED APPROACH (HRBA)

The CDE will endeavour to apply a HRBA in its operations. Four main focus areas need to be addressed:

(a) Vulnerable groups:

- Development efforts need to consciously include vulnerable, disadvantaged or excluded groups.

- Development should pay attention to structural and indirect forms of vulnerability and discrimination in terms of public policies, local power structures or cultural practices.

- Strategies should highlight not only what is done and who is reached, but also what is not done and those who are excluded.

(b) Root causes of poverty, deprivation and human rights violations:

- Development programs must describe a situation not simply in terms of needs, but in terms of society's obligation to respond to the rights of individuals.

- Approaches must be comprehensive and consider the full range of rights. This will form the basis for establishing priorities.

- Development should not only target economic growth, but also expand peoples' capacity to exercise their rights and freedoms.

(c) The relationship between rights-holders and duty-bearers:

- There must be a conscious recognition of beneficiaries as rights-holders and their ability to act on their rights should be targeted.

- Development efforts should seek to install legal and administrative procedures that strengthen accountability and make it possible for ordinary people to claim their rights.

(d) Empowerment:

- Development must include beneficiaries, stakeholders and partners when strategies and goals are determined.

- Participation should not only be regarded as a tool, but also as a goal for development.

- Accountability is not only a concern for the outcome of development, but also for the process by which it is achieved. The organizations involved in implementing development must be accountable to better augment trust and ongoing empowerment.

- Development should promote platforms and networks to support peoples' ability to take part in governance and claim their rights individually and as a group.

4. ESTABLISHING THE CDE

To initiate the formation of a CDE, an extensive public involvement is needed with as many citizens, stakeholders, and Government members as possible. This is a primary process that will continue in the future to ensure the ongoing involvement of all partners in planning and enabling key CDE processes. Maintaining an open dialogue will be a crucial factor for the success of the CDE

The following activities will be needed to initiate the CDE:

- Community Group Presentations

- Open House CDE Future Scenarios

- Focus Group Meetings with stakeholders

- The CDE Community Planning Survey

(a) Community Group Presentations

To ensure that the CDE will be effective and to facilitate ongoing buy-in from the community, the community needs to be involved in the formation process. 'Envision the Community Future' will be a series of workshops conducted for the community residents to develop a shared vision for the CDE. The objective of these workshops is to involve the community in the formation of the CDE and to eliminate possible obstacles. These seminars will also be helpful in understanding the context and characteristics of individual communities.

(b) Open House CDE Future Scenarios

Possible scenarios could be developed for the directions of CDE and to identify how proposed policies will impact the community. A series of open house seminars or a possible virtual open house process could be implemented, and the feedback of the community could be used to attain the best possible direction for the CDE.

(c) Focus Group Meetings with Stakeholders

Focus group meetings could be held with community stakeholders with expertise to understand how best to shape the daily activities of the community. Also, it is important to gain feedback from governmental institution officials who are familiar with particular policy areas. A series of focus groups are needed to achieve a full spectrum vision for the future direction of the CDE.

(d) Community Planning Survey

A survey would be conducted amongst the people of the community to gather an overall public opinion about the future of the CDE with regards to especially relevant aspects of sustainable development programs.

5. CUTTING OF THE CDES

A crucial factor for the success of the CDE approach is the definition of the size of the CDEs. Instability could be caused by either establishing CDEs that are too broad, or by establishing CDEs that are too small. Every conflict zone comes from an individual context with many sensitive factors. As such, effective research to determine the appropriate size for a respective CDE in a conflict zone will be critical and will largely depend on the particular circumstances of that conflict zone.

Through research the following factors will be evaluated to determine the best cut for the CDEs in each conflict situation:

- Economic Autarky

- Political Stability

- Cultural Homogeneity

(a) Economic Autarky

Economic prosperity is mainly dependent on international trade. In most conflict zones the economy is devastated. Most crucially, the infrastructure that brings basic goods and services to the individual is not in place, so the needs of the people cannot be met. For conflict zones, international trade cannot be the first step because they are not competitive on the world market, generally due to distortion of the local currency and interruption of production of local exports. Those regions should begin the rebuilding process with economic protection and autarky (at least in some industries). However, the extent of economic protection cannot be limited to an area that is too small otherwise there will not be the appropriate economies of scale for the provision of necessary goods and services.

(b) Political Stability

The political stability of a conflict zone is contingent on several factors. It is primarily connected to the domestic political situation of the conflict zone, but is also heavily influenced by the international perception of the conflict and the state's relevant relationships with other states. Assessing how stable a conflict zone is, and then assessing where the particular political instability stems from will be a key part of understanding the best form of CDE for that area.

(c) Cultural Homogeneity

Conflict can be intensified if the affected state is fragmented on a cultural, racial or religious level. A careful assessment of the homogeneity of the population will be vital to ensure that the CDE concept is applied appropriately. Researching this aspect of a conflict zone will help to shape the CDE and figure out the best cut for a given area.

VII
PRINCIPLES AND POLICY

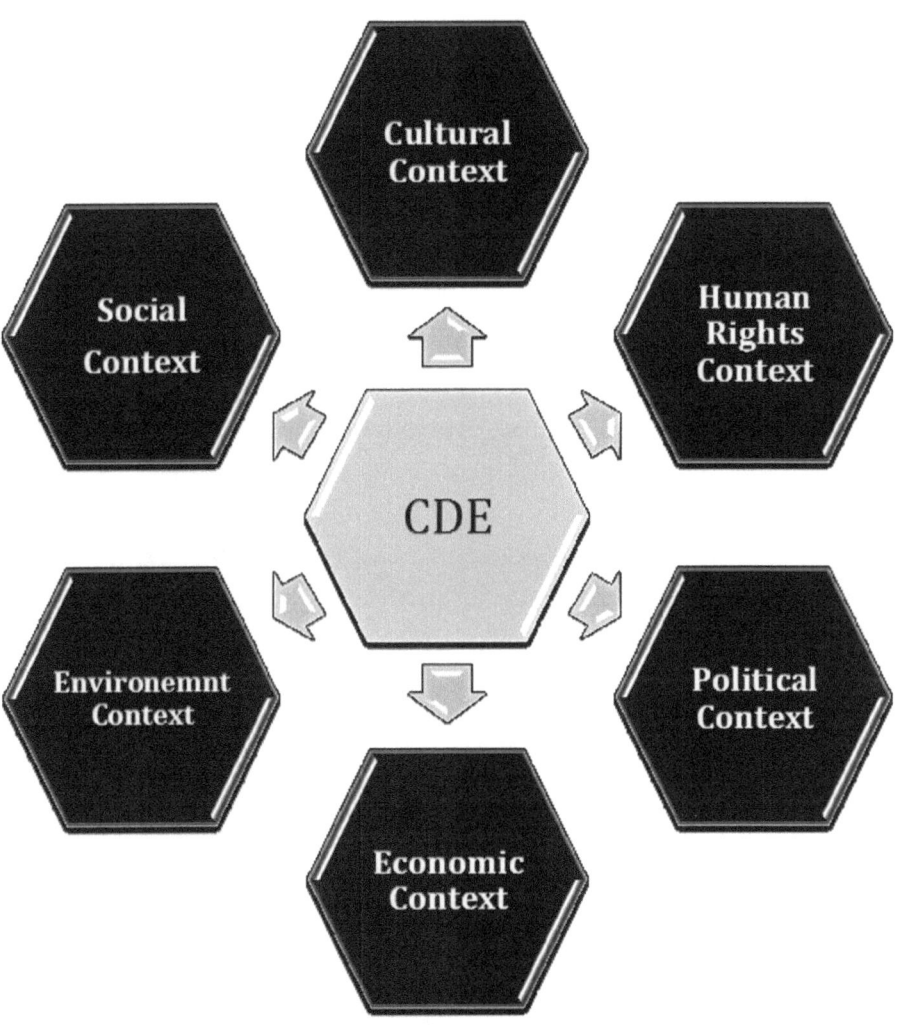

1. GUIDING PRINCIPLES

There are five guiding principles that underlie the CDE concept. The principles operate on the presumption of 'accountability' (detailed in the following section).

(a) Good Governance

The goal of establishing CDEs is to actively promote effective and participative systems of governance on all levels of society. By promoting good governance CDEs can engage peoples' creativity, energy and diversity. Promoting Good Governance also carries the obligation to establish administrative efficiency and ensure that objectives can be met in a timely manner.

(b) Popular Participation

The CDE concept will ensure that participation is active, free and meaningful — extending to the inclusion of civil society, minorities, women, children and others. By establishing CDEs, the diverse needs of all people in existing and future communities will aim to be met. In addition, personal wellbeing, social cohesion and inclusion will be promoted and equal opportunities will be created. Popular Participation contains the broad goal to empower societies to develop in such a way that is most beneficial to them. People need to have the capacities and access to improve their communities and influence their own lives.

(c) Sustainable Development

Establishing CDEs will help to build sustainable economies, which will continue to provide prosperity and opportunities.

CDEs will be designed to place environmental and social costs on those who impose them and to operate within relevant resource and environmental constraints. In the establishment and operation of CDEs, the implications of using resources on future generations will be carefully considered.

(d) Effective Policy

CDEs will ensure that policy is developed and implemented on the basis of strong empirical evidence. A precautionary approach will be adopted and public attitudes and values will be strongly considered. A key advantage of the CDE concept is that it is adaptable and can mould to the characteristics of individual communities. Creating effective policy that reflects the needs of different societies is a crucial element of CDEs.

(e) Human Rights

The CDE concept will expressly apply a HRBA in its establishment and operation. Development goals will be framed in terms of the relevant international human rights commitments of the state — as legally enforceable entitlements on a national level. This necessarily includes:

- Explicitly taking human rights obligations into account at every stage of national and local development processes (from the identification of needs through to policy and program identification, as well as implementation, monitoring and evaluation).

- Addressing the full spectrum of indivisible, interdependent and interrelated rights: civil, political, cultural, economic and social.

- Ensuring that all sectors of national planning reflect the human rights framework (for example, health, education, housing, justice administration and political participation).

- Building the capacity of public representatives, civil servants and local officials so that they apply the human rights framework in their work (e.g., through recruitment, training and specialized advice).

- To address discrimination as a priority and protect vulnerable groups.

2. ACCOUNTABILITY

Accountability is a fundamental facet of the CDE concept. All operations will be transparent, and information regarding CDE activities will be easily accessible. The CDE will base its activities on performance indicators, as well as empirical audit accounting.

(a) Performance

Proven performance is about demonstrating what the CDE has done and explaining the added value of its work. In order to achieve outcomes, it is essential to have clear objectives. Reflecting on objectives and clarifying them through experience will allow the CDE to become certain about exactly what it is trying to achieve in each context. Creating an open dialogue between objectives and performance indicators will be a process that is unique to the CDE concept.

Objectives will be clarified according to the individual needs of communities and an analysis of the characteristics of their social, economical and historical background. Once objectives are clarified, performance indicators will be necessarily established based on what if required to attain impact and ongoing effectiveness. On an assessment of performance the objectives will then be able to be tweaked to better fit the evolving situation in a given context. This open narrative between objectives and performance will ensure that the best approach can be made towards the needs of communities.

(b) Auditing

The CDE business plan must connect the financial realities of an enterprise community with broader sustainable development objectives and a HRBA. In order to ensure performance the CDE will have three official audits: a Human Rights Audit, a Social Audit and a Financial Audit. Regular social management and human rights accounts considered alongside financial accounts will give continuous, integrated management information so that the CDE can better achieve its goals. Reading the audits together will give an overall picture of the value of the CDE. As such, social and economic performance will be carefully tuned in with financial performance.

- Human Rights Audit: This audit will assess the CDE's compliance with human rights obligations and ensure that the CDE is consistently applying a HRBA to all its activities.

- Social Audit: This process will allow the CDE to monitor and evaluate its performance and continue to adjust its objectives accordingly. The social audit will be a key part of the CDE's open dialogue between assessing performance and evolving objectives.

- Financial Audit: A financial audit will necessarily take place to ensure the continued viability and functionality of the CDE as an ongoing project.

This feature sets the CDE concept apart from other development projects that are predominantly connected to only one major element. By creating a framework whereby the CDE is accountable on several levels, the CDE initiative introduces a more integrated approach towards conflict zones.

(c) Transparency

Transparency is a key element of the CDE concept's commitment to accountability. Establishing CDEs in conflict zones will necessarily include fostering fairness and a transparent environment by establishing relevant bodies to enforce transparency, accountability and fairness in all CDE activities. Moreover, corruption will be alleviated through the assignment of a taskforce responsible for assessing any corruption allegations. This taskforce will be the official body responsible for anti-corruption measures, and will also serve as the first point of contact for reporting cases and investigations.

VIII
FINAL NOTE

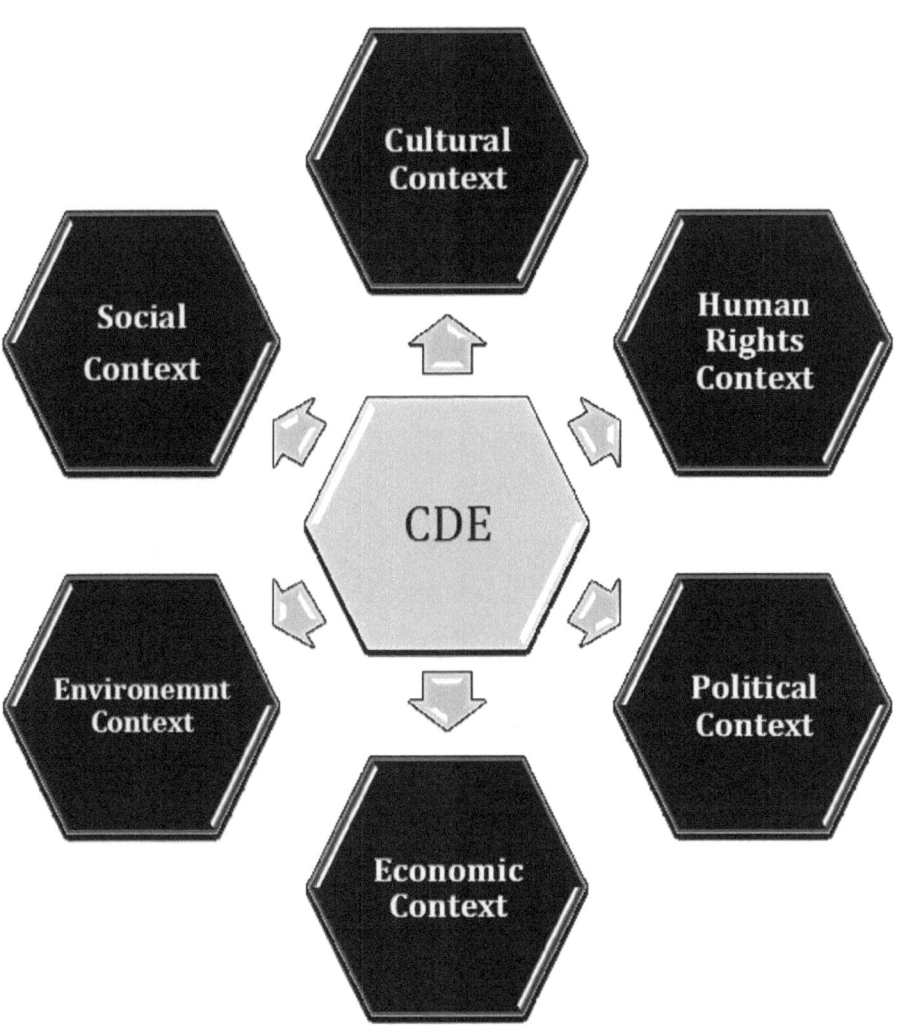

Conflict resolution is by no means a simple problem to solve. Rather, it is multifaceted and influenced by several factors. These can be as straightforward as an incompatibility of goals or as complex as a long standing ethnic or religious disagreement. Conflict is largely characterized by the context in which it exists and colored by the unique political and historical features of a given nation-state. Conflict zones are further complicated by already existing attempts to resolve the conflict as well as the disposition of the people most affected by the conflict. With these factors in mind, any endeavour to appease conflict zones must carefully travese social, cultural and economic issues (amongst others). Ultimately, conflict presents a difficult picture that must be carefully and appropriately approached.

The CDE concept proposes a solution to conflict that meets a cross between decentralization and microbusiness models. A defining attribute of the CDE concept is its focus on the people most affected by the conflict. By shifting conflict resolution away from a solution that is merely political, the CDE aims to provide a solution that will be real and durable. The formation of a CDE will be backed by extensive research and shaped by the needs of the individuals in a given community. The CDE will be facilitated by the ICRG, which will engage with comprehensive research and seek valuable partnerships. This will provide a complete framework in which the CDE can fully function. The task is ambitious but the CDE concept introduces a fresh look at conflict that forces resolution to be directed away from traditional political methods. Instead, the CDE presents a conflict resolution method that will be sustainable because it will be well augmented and directed by the individuals most affected by the conflict themselves.

www.ingramcontent.com/pod-product-compliance
Lightning Source LLC
Chambersburg PA
CBHW050339290526
45785CB00006B/2557